United We Stan

A Musical

Ken Bolam, Roy Oakes
and Les Scott

Samuel French – London
New York – Sydney – Toronto – Hollywood

CHARACTERS

Mick ⎫
Eagle ⎮
Robbo ⎬ The Gang
Kath ⎮
Jane ⎭

Mr Stewart ⎫
Mrs Stewart ⎮
Mrs Carter ⎬ The Parents
Mrs Williams ⎭

Jitters, the butler
Gossip
Mr Foreman, youth club leader
Mr McGrath, football manager
Secretary, to Mr McGrath
Radio Presenter
TV Producer
Roger, a TV interviewer
Liz, a sound engineer
Bob, a camera person
Christine, a clapperboard operator
Newspaper Reporter
TV Presenter
TV Crew
Crowd in Town Centre
Football Supporters

The action centres around the town of Merton, somewhere north of Newport Pagnell

Time—the present

United We Stand was first presented at St John's RC School, London, E13, in March 1982, by the "SJS Theatre Workshop", before going on tour to several fringe venues, including the Theatre Royal, Stratford East and The Tramshed in Woolwich, with the following cast of characters

Mick	⎫	Barry Fink
Eagle	⎪	Peter Stuart
Robbo	⎬ The Gang	Anthony Lynch
Kath	⎪	Diane Watson
Jane	⎭	Delores Fredericks
Mr Stewart	⎫	Billy Edwards
Mrs Stewart	⎬ The Parents	Sharon Cass
Mrs Carter	⎪	Maureen Louis
Mrs Williams	⎭	Selena Dupuy
Gossip		Jennifer Lockhart
Mr Foreman, youth club leader		Michael Graves
Mr McGrath, football manager		Jerry Gujadhur
TV Producer		Nicholas Graves
TV Interviewer/Presenter		Simon McGrath
Sound Engineer		Robert Johnson
Camera Operator		David Revell
Jitters, the butler		Michael Cordina
Secretary		Louise Marius
Clapper		Janet Russie
TV Crew, Crowd, Football Supporters etc.		Company

Musical Director: Ken Bolam
Choreography: Sarah Harwood
Produced and directed by Mark Pattenden

MUSICAL NUMBERS

ACT I

Music 1	**Overture**	Instrumental
Music 2	**United We Stand**	Company
Music 3	**To Coin a Phrase**	Mr and Mrs Stewart and Mick
Music 4	**Engaged Tone**	Kath and Jane
Music 5	**Mark Our Words**	Mrs Carter, Mrs Stewart, Mrs Williams, Jane and Kath
Music 6	**Down Our Way**	Jane, Kath and Company

ACT II

Music 7	**Overture** (Reprise)	Instrumental
Music 8	**Downbeat Mess**	Company
Music 9	**Downbeat Mess** (Variation)	Jane
Music 10	**Strobo Jive**	Instrumental
Music 11	**Look Before You Leap**	Mick and Jane
Music 12	**Better Give Over**	Company
Music 13	**Finale**	Company

The vocal score is available separately from Samuel French Ltd

There are no orchestral parts for *United We Stand* but full orchestrated backing tracks are available from Ken Bolam. Please contact Samuel French Ltd for further details.

AUTHORS' NOTE

In producing *United We Stand*, directors should constantly be aware of the style of the play, which is very light and almost on the lines of a stage version of television situation comedy. This allows for the development of some lively cameo roles.

A link with a local football club may help the cast to build belief in a real football team. In the original production the school had the support of West Ham United and the cast met the players and the manager, as well as going to training sessions. Needless to say, Merton United's colours were claret and blue.

STAGING

If the budget is to be kept to a minimum a simple wooden booth with two book flats can be used. In the original production the booth had a curtain and opening doors which added change possibilities. Other basic units which were used were four black drama rostra (used for levels, launderette machine, commentator's desk, etc.), two tables (used in the living-room, launderette and football manager's office), eight chairs and a long bench for the football terracing.

THE FLOOR PLAN

The flats were covered in brick effect wallpaper and the booth was black, with black drapes and curtains.

It opened to a painted interior which formed the backcloth for the Stewarts' living-room and the football manager's office. The front of the doors, which were visible when the curtains were not drawn, had a painted scene of Merton United's main gates, which was used as the audience came in, with a single high-mounted spot on, as well as in the play.

The booth was a single rectangle of 2×1 with a side piece to aid stability. When the doors were open the back had to be weighted.

This simple set, with a minimum of movable parts, led to slick change-overs between scenes and was very portable.

LIGHTING

The only special effects required are a mirrorball for the disco and a stroboscope for ACT II, SCENE 2. The use of followspots will add atmosphere, especially during the songs.

An LP record of *United We Stand*, by the Original Cast, is available on Royal Records No. PPC 102, distributed by Stage 2 Records. We would be grateful if Producers would include this information in their programme notes.

For my Dad
K.B.

Other musicals by the same authors:

Rockafella
School's Out

ACT I

Music 1. Overture (optional)

The terraces of Merton United FC

When the CURTAIN *rises the Company are seated, but as they begin the song
"United We Stand" they rise to their feet. This is a full cast number with the
stage a sea of the chosen football colours; scarves, banners, flags, etc. The chant
at the beginning of the song can take place in darkness with a slow fade and the
Lights up to full when the band start playing*

Music 2. United We Stand

Company (*whispering*) United, United, United we stand.
United, United, United we stand.
United, United, United we stand.
(*Singing*) United, United we stand.
United, United we stand.

When a town is divided,
When life gets one-sided,
United, United we stand!
When you have to take sides,
When there's nowhere to hide,
United, United we stand!

United, United, United we stand.
Don't stand by,
You'll get by when
United we stand.

When you have to call bluff,
When enough is enough,
United, United we stand!
To stand up for a right
We'll show all our might.
United, United we stand!

United, United, United we stand.
Don't stand by,
You'll get by when
United we stand.

United, United, United we stand.

At the end of the song the tables, chairs etc. for Scene 2 *are brought on*

Scene 2

The living-room of Mr and Mrs Stewart. Saturday afternoon of the quarter-final. Nearly 5 p.m.

The Lights come up on Mick and his father Mr Stewart who are sitting at the table. Mr Stewart is putting new batteries into a transistor radio

Mr Stewart Fine time this picked to conk out.

Mick You're telling me. Oh, come on, Dad, we could have had the telly warmed up by now. The suspense is killing me. I want to know if they've hung on.

Mr Stewart I only wish we'd been able to get tickets but it only holds thirty-five thousand, that ground.

Mick By! You've changed your tune. I usually have to twist your arm to go to away games.

Mr Stewart Well, Mick, sixth round of the Cup, what do you expect? It doesn't happen every day.

Mick Or every year or even every decade! For heaven's sake, Dad.

Mr Stewart Don't worry, they'll hold out all right. One up by half-time — they'll have scored a couple more by now.

Mick And we'll never know about it.

Mrs Stewart enters smiling happily

Mrs Stewart They're through.

Mr Stewart How do you know? When did you hear?

Mrs Stewart I just knew they had it in them.

Mick Have they won?

Mrs Stewart Won? What do you mean?

Mick What do I mean? What do you mean?

Mrs Stewart They're through. Those hyacinth bulbs I put under the bed, they've come through.

Mr Stewart Come through the bed?

Mrs Stewart No, silly, they've come through, the shoots, they're through. They'll be nice flowers soon.

Mick Hyacinths! We thought you meant United were through.

Mrs Stewart You daft things. Tut! Merton United! How would I know how they went on, I've been working in the kitchen all afternoon, not fiddling about with radios and worrying about football.

She exits

Mr Stewart Don't bother saying anything, Mick. They just don't understand. (*Returning to the radio*) It looked so simple when Robert Donat was fiddling with one in that picture about Marconi.

Mick For heaven's sake . . .

The radio crackles into life

Mr Stewart Get me my coupon from the drawer, will you?

Mick It's the only draw you're likely to get. (*He rises and fetches the coupon*)

Radio Presenter And here is Colin Batey with your classifed check.

Mr Stewart They're on. Quick, sit down. United'll be one of the first.

Radio Presenter The FA Cup sixth round. Arsenal two, West Ham United two. Birmingham City nil, Manchester United three. Norwich City one, Merton United two.

Mick ⎱ (*together*) ⎰ They've done it, we're through.
Mr Stewart ⎰   ⎱ Yes! Semi-finals, who would have believed it?

They leap about excitedly. The results continue in the background

Mrs Stewart enters

Mrs Stewart Have they won by any chance?

Mick Course they have.

Mr Stewart I knew it, I knew they'd do it. I feel so happy I feel like paying the back rent.

Mrs Stewart You're like a pair of kids. Perhaps we can have a bit of peace now it's all over with.

Mick All over? It's only just started. We'll have to get tickets for the semi.

Mr Stewart Semi? What about Wembley?

Mick Hey, I hope it's on the telly tonight.

Mrs Stewart Oh no. I suppose I'm going to have to miss the film again tonight, am I?

Mr Stewart It's only on for an hour.

Mrs Stewart An hour? It'll not be worth bothering by then. I can't see what all the fuss is about; eleven grown men trying to get a piece of leather filled with air between two sticks.

Mr Stewart Turn the radio off, Mick, the poor fellow can't compete with your mother when she's in full flight. I'll check my coupon tomorrow.

Mick turns off the radio

Mrs Stewart Haven't you done that? What if my numbers have come up?

Mick I thought you didn't like football.

Mrs Stewart The pools is different. We might win a million pounds.

Mr Stewart No, somebody has got to win, but it won't be us.

Mrs Stewart What's the sense in sending them in then? You've got to be an optimist.

Mr Stewart I am an optimist. There doesn't seem to be much point being anything else these days. Besides what's a pessimist except an optimist who knows all the facts.

Mrs Stewart You've got to keep trying, Dad—someone has to win.

Mick Yeah, and who's to say it won't be us. Think of it, having all that money—you can win a million pounds on the pools. You can do anything with money.

Mr Stewart If you believe you can have anything you want if you have money, that means you haven't got any. A million . . . a couple of thousand would do me. Just to put in the Halifax to help us keep the wolf from the door.

Mrs Stewart Yes, things are tight today. These days money costs too much.
My dad always used to say that.

Mick (*laughing*) You what? Money costs too much?

Mr Stewart (*lighting a pipe*) Your mother may have a point there, Michael.
Money today is tainted.

Mick Yeah, taint yours and taint mine.

Mr Stewart No, listen, son. When it comes to money, believe me everybody
is of the same religion. When a bloke tells you it isn't the money it's the
principle of the thing—believe me, it's the money.

Mick You talk about money as if it's a bad thing to have a lot. Well, you can
give me the luxuries of life and I'd gladly give up the necessities.

Mr Stewart Oh yes, that would suit you fine, wouldn't it, wallowing like a pig
in a trough of luxury? You'd love not having to work for a living.

Mick I wouldn't be lazy, I'd work. Invest my money and double it on the
Stock Exchange or in business.

Mr Stewart Listen—the only way to double your money these days is to fold
it in two and put it in your pocket. Things are bad everywhere, it's not as if I
don't want to win the pools. I do! It's just that I wouldn't like to win as
much as a million. Just enough to put in the building society so that life
wasn't such a matter of survival. By God, when I was a lad, a man who
used to save money was called a miser—today he's a bloody wonder.

Mrs Stewart My dad always used to say that the worst thing about money
was that the poor who needed it most, never had it.

Mr Stewart (*exasperatedly*) Well, your father would say something like that,
wouldn't he? I've never heard such a load of nonsense—the poor who need
money the most never had it. Your dad was flippin' looney.

Mick (*laughing*) Well we're not exactly poor but just think what it would be
like to win the pools—win a lot, I mean.

*The upper-class family dream sequence begins. Mick and Mr and Mrs Stewart
can adopt twenties-style freeze poses as if caught in a photograph*

*Jitters, the butler, enters. He is ridiculously old and carries a tray which has a
glass glued to it. He starts to shuffle his way across the stage*

Mick Oh, the Chancellor of the Exchequer phoned this morning when you
were out.

Mr Stewart Did he now. And what did he have to say for himself?

Mick Well, he was sounding us out for another loan to the Government. He
said they'd pay us back and that that was the truth this time.

Mr Stewart The truth! Ha, a politician only tells the truth once in his career
and then immediately repents.

Mrs Stewart Well, one little loan wouldn't do any 'arm. If we got it back like,
with interest 'course!

Mick Why don't you check their credit, Pater, how much do they owe us up
to present?

Mrs Stewart Yarse, check the tick-book, it's on the table by the door.

*Mr Stewart goes to the table R, passing Jitters on the way who is still painfully
making his way out*

Mr Stewart (*looking in the tick-book*) Ah, here we are.

Mr Stewart walks back across the room to his wife, ignoring Jitters once again

Mr Stewart Fifty million.

Mrs Stewart Quid! Oh I don't know about a loan for them slackers.

Mr Stewart Yes, they do seem a bit risky. God loves the poor, otherwise he
   wouldn't have created so many of them, but he also loves the rich,
   otherwise he wouldn't have distributed so much between so few of us.

Mick Admirable sentiment, Father, well said. I say do you have the odd five
   pound note in your pocket, I want to light a cigarette?

Mr Stewart You know me, I never carry loose change.

Mrs Stewart I don't know why, it's money hafter hall.

   Jitters tucks the tray and glass under his arm and finally makes his exit as:

*The first chords of "To Coin A Phrase" strike up. This can be sung in Fagan
style*

Music 3. To Coin A Phrase

Mr Stewart ⎫ Find it in the vaults of Banks,
Mrs Stewart ⎬ Dollars, pound notes, roubles, francs,
Mick ⎭ Your standard of living they enhance.
   Save it for a rainy day,
   Save it for a holiday
   To Corfu, Cornwall or the South of France.

   Gamble it all if you like,
   Even spend some on the wife,
   On people you know for a slap-up meal.
   Let it go to your head,
   Sleep with it in the bed,
   Some to get it they will even steal.

(*Chorus*) It makes you, it breaks you,
   Directs you or it takes you.
   There's absolutely nothing you can do.
   Despise it, desire it,
   Avoid or fraternize it,
   To coin a phrase we all need slips
   Of green and blue.

(*Repeat chorus*)

   You can buy a football team,
   Realize a long-lost dream,
   Have an operation on your broken nose.
   Buy a car, or chain of shops,
   Own Miss Selfridge if you want,
   Get yourself some handy dandy clothes.

   Some folks even kill for it,
   Change their name to Eartha Kitt,

Do the strangest things for those wads of green.
For your information, we're the same denomination,
I guess you know exactly what I mean.

It makes you, it breaks you,
Directs you or it takes you.
There's absolutely nothing you can do.
Despise it, desire it,
Avoid or fraternize it,
To coin a phrase we all need slips
Of green and blue,
Green and blue,
Green and blue.

At the end of the song they retake their places around the table and make as if snapping out of the dream. Mr Stewart starts to light his pipe

Mrs Stewart Are you staying in tonight then, Mick?
Mick No, I'm going to the youth club first. Eagle and Robbo should be back from Norwich, so I can hear all about it.
Mrs Stewart Eagle?
Mick Yes, Ronnie Churchill. Eagle's his nickname.
Mrs Stewart Eagle, indeed. What a name! I was watching a programme on the telly the other night with that David Attenborough. It was about the life of the Eagle and the . . . (*She pauses to think*) Oh, what do they call it? It's like a South American eagle. The er—er—er . . . (*She gazes off trying to remember*)
Mr Stewart (*puffing on his pipe, like the TV advert*) Condor!

Mick and Mrs Stewart laugh

CURTAIN

SCENE 3

A room in a youth club. Saturday evening

There are two tables with chairs. On top of one of the tables are some books and perhaps a telephone and directory

When the CURTAIN *rises Mr Foreman, the youth club leader, sits behind the table* R *which has books on it. He is a youthful, optimistic figure, full of beaming smiles and godliness. A group of young people: Eagle, Robbo, Mick, Kath and Jane, are seated at the other table—some on chairs, others on the table itself*

Eagle Mick, you should have seen it. We were incredible. There were thousands of us.
Robbo Thousands of us.
Eagle They marched us all together in a big gang, from the station; it was amazing!
Robbo Thousands of us.

Mick What did they play like, Eagle?

Eagle Great! We were singing and chanting all the way through.

Kath (*moaning*) It was ever so noisy, Jane. All those people.

Robbo Thousands of us.

Mick What were the goals like.

Robbo Same as they are at our ground, only with orange nets.

Mick The goals we scored, Robbo.

Kath I didn't see any of the goals.

Jane How did you know what the score was, Kath?

Kath Everybody in our end went berserk twice. I was just shoved and pushed around. What an experience! I thought I was going to get crushed to death at one stage. I saw the ball go up in the air a few times and that was about it.

Eagle It was great, Mick. Pity you and your old man couldn't get tickets.

Mick We'll be at the semi-final.

Eagle Yeah, Villa Park against Leeds. They're as hard as they come.

Mick (*smiling at him*) The team is pretty hard as well. Leeds are a good side and they'll not be short of support.

Robbo Thousands of them.

Jane You know, I don't think this lot are going to talk about anything else for the next few weeks. I was afraid you might have been infected as well, Kath, after this afternoon.

Kath You're joking. If you think I'm going to another football match with you, Eagle, you've got another think coming. It's daft.

Eagle Just listen to her, lads, football daft. Why am I going out with this girl? I treat her to the experience of a lifetime and what do I get in return?

Kath The only reason I went was because that was the first time you'd asked me out for a fortnight.

Eagle Yes, but it was all the way to Norwich.

Kath You didn't even sit next to me on the bus on the way back. I had to sit with Robbo and all he ever said was "thousands of 'em".

Robbo Well, there were.

Jane Were what?

Mick Thousands of 'em. (*He laughs*)

Jane Oh, don't you start!

Kath I tell you, Eagle, this football thing is driving me bonkers. It wasn't so bad last year when they weren't doing so well, but now it's all you ever go on about. Sometimes I think you hardly notice me. (*She stands and smoothes down her skirt, showing off her figure*)

Eagle Sometimes I think all you want in a boyfriend is a bloke who'll walk you in the park, be polite, respectful and clean living.

Kath So?

Mick You won't find anybody like that now that Albert Schweitzer's dead.

Robbo Who?

Mick Don't worry, Robbo, he used to play for Bayern Munich.

Kath They're off about football again—let's go and have a talk with Mr Foreman and leave these.

The lads continue talking sotto voce as Kath and Jane join Mr Foreman at the other table

Mr Foreman Hello, girls. I hear you went to the match this afternoon, Kath.

Kath Oh, don't you start as well. We've come over here to get away from football.

Jane Yeah, they're driving us mad. They talk about nothing else.

Mr Foreman Come on, Jane. United are doing well and it's nice for the lads to have a bit of success.

Kath Oh, we know, but we get it morning, noon and night. My mother's threatened to put her foot through the telly if Dad dares to turn it on tonight.

Jane They don't even think about girls any more. I haven't been asked out by a lad for a month. I heard rumours that Micky Stewart was going to ask me for a date but I suppose I shall have to wait till the cricket season.

Kath It's the same for me with Eagle.

Mr Foreman Well, it might be appropriate for Botham to ask you out in the cricket season—get it?

Jane ⎫
Kath ⎭ (*together*) No.

Mr Foreman Botham—both of them. I'll keep cracking that joke till I get it.

Kath Seriously though, Mr Foreman, we might as well just stay home until the football season's over.

Mr Foreman What you've got to do, girls, is to make the lads start to think.

Jane With Robbo, impossible. (*She laughs*)

Kath Ssh! What do you mean, sir?

Mr Foreman Familiarity breeds contempt. A bit of male competition for girls such as you two and the others that would shake Eagle and Mick into action.

Kath But we get the same crowd of lads in here every week and they all talk about football.

Mr Foreman Listen—I was chatting to the youth leader of St John's the other night and he was telling me the girls there feel like doing something different. So what I was thinking about was a disco, a joint bop. Invite St John's down here. If Mick and Eagle perhaps see some of St John's lads taking an interest in you two it could well prompt them into action, so to speak.

Jane Hey, that sounds like a good idea.

Kath Yeah. Sir, could we do that?

Mr Foreman Why not? What about in a fortnight's time?

Kath Yes, on the Saturday.

Mr Foreman It could be easily arranged. Shall we go and tell the lads?

They move across to Eagle, Mick and Robbo

Mick I tell you, if he could get into shooting positions more often, he'd score a load of goals.

Mr Foreman Now, gentlemen, let's forget football for a minute. How would you fancy a joint disco with St John's here a fortnight tonight?

Eagle (*after a pause*) Suppose so.

Mick So that's what you've been cooking up over there.

Eagle Heh, wait a minute, that's semi-final day. We'll be at Villa Park.

Kath I might have known it.

Jane They can't forget football for two minutes.

Mr Foreman Now wait a minute. You'll be back by eight o'clock, won't you?

Mick We should be. Be a nice idea, we can celebrate reaching Wembley.

Kath That's not the point of the disco.

Mr Foreman No, but then if we have the disco, everyone will be happy and that's what we are here for. Kath, Jane?

Kath ⎫ (*together*) ⎧ Yes, all right.
Jane ⎭   ⎩ Okay.

Robbo What are we having St John's for? Whose clever idea was it to invite them?

Mr Foreman Mine.

Robbo Excellent idea.

Jane And perhaps there'll be some boys there who are not just interested in football. (*She pauses*) Did you hear me, Michael Stewart?

Eagle Ooh, she's getting at you now, Mick.

Mick Actually, Jane, I mean I don't know whether this is the right time or place in front of everybody . . .

Jane Go on, go on.

Mick Well, there's something I've always found difficult to say.

Jane Yes, yes.

Mick But, but I'm going to try and say it now.

Kath nudges Jane

Jane I'm listening.

Mick Okay then. (*He pauses*) Peter Piper picked a peck of pickled pepper.

Jane Stewart, sometimes I don't know why I bother. (*She turns and walks back to the other table*)

Kath You've got no consideration. You've upset her, you rat.

Mick Sorry! I couldn't resist it. Jane, do you want me to walk you home?

Eagle and Robbo wolf-whistle

Jane You needn't bother.

Mick Oh, come on, it was only a joke. (*He walks towards her*) A joke. Come on and get your coat. Y'know, there are times when you look at me, and I could really fancy you and it makes me think . . .

Jane Think what?

Mick Makes me think you'd better hurry or we'll miss *Match of the Day*.

Mick exits

Jane (*quickly following him*) I'm warning you, if you don't . . .

Jane exits

Kath Are you taking me home, Eagle?

Eagle Oh, yes, as long as——

Kath Don't you dare say it!

Eagle As long as I can get a bottle of Coke first.

Kath (*smiling*) Go on then, be quick.

Robbo I want a bottle of belch water as well.

Eagle Well, come on then.

Mr Foreman Hey, before everyone zooms off—if we are going to have a disco here, we'll need you people to bring some of your records along to bolster the collection.

Kath It's all right. I'll bring mine along. Which reminds me, Eagle, how long are you going to have those Four Tops albums of mine?

Eagle Oh, those, yes, well—er—I'll probably drop them in tomorrow.

Kath What time?

Eagle Well, I don't know. Expect me when I come.

Kath I'm going to my sister's tomorrow lunch time and we might stay for tea.

Eagle Well, I'll give you a phone.

Kath Oh yeah, I've heard that one before.

Robbo Heh, come on, are we going to get this Coke or not?

Eagle and Robbo exit

Mr Foreman You see, Kath, you're getting to him. He'll give you a ring.

Kath I'll believe it when it happens, he's said that before and he never phones.

Mr Foreman (*collecting his books off the table*) He could well do tomorrow. Won't be a minute, just going to cash up these memberships.

Mr Foreman exits

Kath I think I'm going to have to teach Eagle how to use a telephone.

Jane enters

Jane and Kath go the table R *with the telephone and directory and sing*

Music 4. Engaged Tone

Jane }
Kath }
Engaged tone, engaged tone,
Rapid pips to tell you
To insert your money.
Hold on till pips stop
Before speaking to me.
You can look me up
In the directory.
Fourteen Baldwin Street,
Eight-two-five-one-two-three.
Maybe someday you will give me a ring.
Maybe someday you'll give me a call.
I'd like to be your connection.
Like us to have that engaged tone.
Engaged tone, engaged tone
Rapid pips to tell you *etc.*
(*Repeat ad lib*)

CURTAIN

SCENE 4

The launderette. A few days later

There is a row of seats facing the audience. Plastic bags full of clothes and packets of washing powder emphasize the setting

When the CURTAIN *rises Jane, Kath and Mrs Stewart are sitting watching the washing going round. The girls' mothers, Mrs Carter and Mrs Williams, are folding some sheets. It is important to create an atmosphere of a "woman's world" and it is in this scene that the seeds for action are sown*

Mrs Carter He's promised me one day he'll buy me an automatic washing machine, then I won't have to come down here.

Mrs Williams You know you'll still come. It's the company, isn't it? By the way, how is your Ron? Is he still trying to lose weight?

Mrs Carter Still trying. Do you know, every night before he gets into bed he strips off and does his exercises. I wouldn't mind so much but last night he did them in front of the window. There he was jumping up and down and the curtains were wide open.

Mrs Williams Aye, what did you say to that?

Mrs Carter I said to him, "Come on, Ron, get to bed, I don't want the neighbours to think I married you for your money."

The three women laugh loudly

Mrs Williams Hey, Kath, never mind just sitting there. Have you put enough powder in that machine?

Kath Course I have, Mother, I'm not daft.

Jane Did Eagle ring you yesterday then?

Kath Did he heck! I rushed back from my sister's, what a waste of time. I bet I never see those records again. Did Mick ask you out when he took you home?

Jane Yeah, we arranged to meet tonight at seven o'clock but then he had to change it to eight because he's got to get his tickets for the semi-final.

Kath I'd tell him where to stuff his date. If picking a ticket up for a football match is more important than going out with you . . . well, I'd tell him straight.

Jane I should have done but then again you should tell Eagle where to get off, Kath.

Kath You're right, it's always easy to tell other people what they should do. I don't even know when I'm going to see him next.

Mrs Williams Oh, are you still on about that boy? Boys and music, that's all she thinks of.

Mrs Stewart Well, Nora, with our Michael it's football, football.

Jane No mention of girls?

Mrs Stewart His dad's just the same. I have to put up with it on the television all the time, even in summer.

Jane Not even one girl?

Mrs Carter Don't mention men and football. I'm sick to death with it. Ron talks to Jane and me about nothing else.

Mrs Stewart Yes, but I've got two of 'em on about it. This season is the worst ever. Just because they're doing well in the Cup they've gone mad.

Mrs Williams It hasn't started yet. Our Arthur's talking about going to Wembley for the final already. I wouldn't mind but until a couple of months ago he hadn't set foot inside Merton United's ground for over ten years and now he tells everybody he's a life-long supporter.

Mrs Carter Yes, Ron is on about Wembley. Says he might make a weekend of it.

Mrs Williams A weekend? And just what will he get up to in London for a weekend?

Mrs Carter Oh, I don't have to worry about my Ron, I trust him like I trust myself. (*She pauses*) Eh, I'd better keep an eye on him.

The women laugh

Mrs Stewart The whole thing is stupid if you ask me. The way they go on. Sometimes in our house you'd think I didn't exist.

Mrs Carter I know what you mean, yet once upon a time Ron and me were like that. (*She holds up her hand and crosses the first two fingers, tapping the index finger on top of the second finger*) I was the nervous one. (*She sighs*) Eeh, it's funny how marriage changes a man.

Mrs Williams Yes, some men think the only thing they owe their wives is a grudge.

Mrs Stewart You've got to treat all the disasters as incidents and none of the incidents as disasters. My father told me that on the day I got married.

Mrs Carter So you'd describe your marriage as one big incident, would you? (*She laughs*) Hey, our Jane, I hope you're taking all this in. Words of wisdom from those who know. And heaven's above, when young people are setting up these days they need all the advice they can get.

All three women nod wisely

Mrs Stewart Yes, it must be really difficult for young marrieds these days.

Mrs Williams Still, one of the biggest stimulants in life is youth and debt.

They all sing "Mark Our Words". This can be sung in typical Country and Western style with all the women doing a country-type dance

Music 5. Mark Our Words

Mrs Carter	Mark our words and lend an ear
Mrs Stewart	To what we have to say
Mrs Williams	It is the truth,
Jane	It is no lie,
Kath	The truth in every way.

We don't know how much to tell you,
Situation is
So very plain.
Why just think with our wombs now

What's the point,
We have a brain.

Now, is it true, Germaine,
What they say about us?
Is it true, maybe,
We can't really say.

Men are mean
It is no lie,
They always have their way.
We do the chores
And scrub the floors
And through the nose we pay.

Scrub the pans
And washday hands
Is all we have to show.
But don't give in,
It is no sin,
Go and tell them no!

We're just around in a man's world,
Only trouble is,
It's been our curse.
Who's to say
We're any better?
What's for sure
We are no worse.

Now is it true, Germaine,
What they say about us?
Is it true, maybe,
We can't really say.

Men are mean
It is no lie,
They always have their way.
We do the chores
And scrub the floors
And through the nose we pay.

Scrub the pans
And washday hands
Is all we have to show.
But don't give in,
It is no sin,
Is no sin,
Is no sin,
Is no sin,
You've got to tell them,

> You've got to tell them,
> Tell them no!

Kath It's all very well you three telling us this, we know what men can be like now.

Mrs Carter Oh, listen to her, you'll have to watch her, she knows what men are like already.

Kath No, I'm serious, Mrs Carter. What you've been saying about your husbands and football is happening to us, just the same.

Jane Yeah, we're being ignored. Kath is supposed to be going out with Eagle, but he's just like all the other lads. At the youth club they talk about nothing but football. He's already broken two dates. That's no way to treat a girl, now is it?

Mrs Williams They're all the same, men. My Arthur would jump off a building just so he could hear an away commentary on hospital broadcasts.

Kath Your Michael's the same with Jane, Mrs Stewart. He keeps saying he'll take her out, then changes his mind. He's just messing her about.

Jane Kath!

Kath But it's true. Sure, there are other lads but they've all gone football daft as well.

Mrs Williams Well, why don't you do something about it? Why not finish with them?

Kath (*annoyed*) You don't finish with Dad, do you?

Mrs Williams Now, Kath, don't be cheeky. What am I supposed to do? Divorce him because he's football daft?

Kath You see, it's the same for us.

Mrs Stewart Well—er—do you know . . . (*She pauses*) . . . I think we should do something about it.

There is a chorus of agreement

Mrs Carter What can we do?

Mrs Stewart We could do what I threatened last night.

The others are agog

Mrs Williams Go on.

Mrs Stewart Well, our Michael came back from a meeting of the supporters' club and he was going on about the television people coming down here to find out how Merton United's Cup run had affected the town. He came in, right in the middle of the Steve McQueen film, woke his father up and the two of 'em kept blabbing on so much that I couldn't even hear. In the end I got up, turned off the telly and shouted at them that I was going to get myself interviewed on this programme and tell them exactly what I thought about Merton United and football.

Mrs Williams You've hit the nail right on the head.

Mrs Carter That's what we'll do.

Jane What programme's it on?

Mrs Stewart I think he said it was *Nationwide*.

Kath We'll get them. We'll tell them just what we think.

Mrs Carter It's not just us though. I was talking to Bessie and Olive this morning and they feel just the same. I'll bet there's plenty more as well.

Mrs Williams We'll have to get the word around.

Mrs Stewart But don't let the men know. I'll work on our Michael and find out exactly when the TV people are coming.

Mrs Williams (*glancing off*) And I know just the person to get the word around. Look who's coming up the street.

Jane Who's that? Look at her hair. You can tell from here it's dyed.

Mrs Carter You know who that is. It's the woman from Number Three Parsonage Street. There's enough peroxide in her hair to disinfect the whole of the House of Commons.

Mrs Williams Just the person we need; tell her something and it gets no further than Tokyo.

Kath How do you know she's coming in here?

Mrs Stewart She can't resist a gossip. If she sees five women in here she'll be in to read out the news. Sit down, come on.

They all sit innocently watching their washing

The Gossip enters. She should have a natural talent for comedy. In the original production the Gossip was a larger-than-life West Indian lady who made her entrance, winged glasses, headscarf, shopping trolley and all, through the audience. She walks up to the women and folds her arms

Gossip I saw you sitting here. I just thought I'd pop in and let you know about poor Alf Tabbinor.

Mrs Carter What is it, pet?

Gossip (*glancing to either side; furtively*) They reckon it's kidneys. Either that or his bowels.

Mrs Carter No, listen. He's been in a bad way. They had to call the doctor out in the middle of the night. Course, it didn't surprise me. I was just saying to Emma Curtin the other day how sallow he looked. It's a sure sign of kidneys.

Mrs Williams Hey, Edith, you know Merton United——

Gossip Don't mention Merton United to me. I heard the other day that one of the player's wives has stopped going to the games. Apparently the other players' wives have been passing rumours about her. You'd think they'd have more sense.

Mrs Carter Listen, we've got something to tell you. Of course, we know with you it won't go any further.

Gossip As God is my witness!

Mrs Carter Well . . .

They close in together as—

the Curtain *falls*

SCENE 5

A street corner. A few days later. Morning

When the CURTAIN *rises Mick and Robbo stand waiting for Eagle*

Robbo Can't wait for the semi-final. Just think, Merton United playing at Villa Park. And us on the telly this morning as well. It's like living a piece of history.

Mick You're feeling poetic this morning, aren't you?

Robbo It inspires me. Merton United versus Leeds in the semi-final of the Cup. Makes me want to do things I've never done before.

Mick Next thing you know, you'll be revising your autobiography to include yourself.

Robbo My auto-what?

Mick (*staring at him*) Do you know, Robbo, my 'ole fruit, I was reading in a paper the other day that the average human only uses fifty percent of his brain potential throughout his life.

Robbo Really? What does he do with the other three quarters?

Mick (*looking in despair at Robbo*) They were right, weren't they?

Robbo How did you find out about this television thing this morning?

Mick Supporters' club. Alf Tabbinor told me. They wanted to make sure there were plenty of supporters down there.

Robbo I don't know what I'll say if they ask me anything.

Mick Just smile at 'em, Robbo. Your good looks will be enough.

Robbo It's great, isn't it? To think we're going to be on the telly.

Mick Yeah, but remember there'll be a lot of other people there as well. You're not going to be the star attraction. And if Eagle doesn't come soon we'll not even be part of the supporting bill.

Robbo brings a comb out of his pocket and starts to comb his hair

What's got into you then, combing your hair?

Robbo Well, there's going to be cameras, isn't there? We're going to be on the telly, aren't we?

Mick I don't know. Get a grip, Robbo. Mention the chance of being on telly and it goes to your head.

Robbo puts away comb and brings out a tie

Robbo You don't think I should wear this then?

Mick I've seen the lot now. A tie!

Robbo You never know, there could be some top producer there, just on the look-out for new talent.

Mick I don't believe this. You should be ashamed of yourself.

Robbo What for?

Mick Well, if you don't know, how can I tell you? Grow up. You're acting like a kid. It's a good job Eagle isn't here, he'd be taking the micky out of you. Boy, would he have a go. He'd make you want to crawl into a hole, he would. He'd rip it out of you something rotten. Combing your hair and bringing a tie!

Eagle enters. He is wearing an overcoat draped over his shoulders, a suit and dark glasses but he still has his Merton United scarf tied round his waist

Eagle Sorry I'm late. We'd better get a move on. It's quite a walk to the set.

Robbo and Mick look at him open-mouthed and amazed

Come on. They'll be waiting for me.

Mick Eagle. You can't be serious.

Eagle (*taking a dramatic pose and speaking in a thespian accent*) Is this the winter of our discontent? Is that serious enough for you? I can play any part, me you know. Ha! ha! just you wait. They'll be pushing contracts under me nose. I'll have to fight 'em off. (*He looks out to the audience as if speaking to someone*) Sorry, Mr Schlesinger, I've just signed up for MGM—better luck next time, huh?

Mick Eagle, don't you think . . . I mean . . . don't you think—(*he sighs*)— you're overdoing it a little?

Eagle You mean the glasses, don't you?

Mick Partly, I mean what would Kath say if she saw you now?

Eagle (*reverting to his normal self*) If last night was anything to go by she would probably have a lot to say. At the moment we're going as steady as a cross-channel ferry. I mentioned football once and she nearly bit my head off.

Mick Could have been worse, but I know what you mean. I had exactly the same treatment off Jane. I was dead excited about the telly coming this morning but as soon as I started talking about it she kept changing the subject. You know something, I think we'd better watch the girls. Believe it or not, I don't think they like football.

Robbo Don't like it? What sort of lives do they lead, then?

Eagle Get away, Mick, they don't really mind or else they'd have said something before now. Come on, let's go, Joe Public awaits me, zoom, zoom, zoom.

Mick Good grief!

They exit as Jane and Kath enter from the opposite side

Kath There they go. Boy, have they got a surprise in store? Just look at the way Eagle's dressed. He never dresses like that for me.

Jane They're really looking forward to it, aren't they? You know, Mick wanted to talk about it all the time last night.

Kath You didn't let him, did you?

Jane No, I did just like you said, but I must admit I began to feel a little bit sorry for him in the end.

Kath Heh, don't you weaken now. United we stand.

They start to exit, following the boys

Jane I know, I know.

They exit   CURTAIN

SCENE 6

The town centre. Later that morning

When the CURTAIN *rises there are a few people upstage watching the television crew set up their equipment. The crew consist of: Roger, an interviewer, Bob, a cameraman, Liz, a sound technician, the Producer, his secretary, and Christine, a clapperboard operator. They must appear very busy throughout*

During the first part of the scene more and more people enter to join the crowd. These must include Mick, Eagle, Robbo, Kath, Jane, Mrs Stewart, Mrs Carter, Mrs Williams, the Gossip and Mr Stewart

Producer (*to Roger*) Roger, I think a good cross section, you know; old, young, both sexes and blar, blar—um—leave it up to you really but keep them short. (*To Bob*) Bob, all right? I'll keep interviewees behind for noddies, then you can get them just before we pack up. Okay on sound, Liz?

Liz nods

Fine, fine. Push it on, everyone, let's have it in the can, then I'll stand everyone drinkies. (*He bustles around*)

Bob (*bored, to Liz*) Drinkies? Some hope of that. Last time the drinks were on him was when a beer barrel fell on him in Aberdeen.

Liz Typical Scorpio. I just knew today would be one big zilch, couldn't be anything else. Who in their right mind would have a Scorpio producer alongside a Capricorn presenter and I'm a Sagittarius and . . . well, it omens bad.

Bob I hate this type of camera.

Liz Don't tell me.

Bob Tell you what?

Liz I can tell, you know; you're a Libra.

Bob (*brightening*) Yes, do you know, it's funny, but the moment I saw you this morning, I just knew. I said to myself, now there's a typical Sagittarius.

Liz Never!

Bob I did, I did!

Liz Well, that's funny, who would believe it? You're into the stars too. Have you read Madame Zsa Zsa this morning?

Bob Foreboding, isn't it?

Liz Yeah, it's going to be one of those days. The sound will be lousy in a place like this. There'll be kids shouting and I bet most of them are Leo's.

Bob Heaven forbid!

Liz And buses coming past all the time. I'll never be able to balance it.

Bob It needs a Libra.

Producer (*to Bob and Liz*) Are you two ready over there if we try a sound test?

Liz Ready as we'll ever be.

Producer (*to Roger*) Okay, Roger, find a body and we'll try the sound.

Roger moves over to the crowd and picks out Robbo

Eagle (*from the crowd*) He's picked Robbo, the only bloke ever to score a penalty with his head.
Producer (*to Robbo*) What's your name?
Robbo (*clearing his throat*) Robbo.
Producer Okay, Ronald, if you would . . .
Robbo It's Robbo!
Producer Right, then, Roger, if you would take Ronald Robbo just over there . .
Roger You don't mind helping us out, do you? Being on TV?

Robbo clears his throat again and starts to peer over Roger's shoulders, looking for the camera

Robbo No, no . . . no.
Producer Roger, ask him some questions for the level.
Roger How old are you, son?
Robbo (*panic stricken, still looking for the camera*) Er—er—er . . .
Liz Louder!

Robbo's mouth opens but nothing comes out

(*Pulling her earphones away from her head*) There's something wrong with these cans, can't hear a ruddy word.

The Producer goes over to Roger and Robbo

Producer You'll have to speak up a bit, sonny, or we'll never get this test done.
Roger (*to Robbo*) Now just relax and speak as loud as you can. We're only doing a test.

Robbo is still looking for the camera. He clears his throat again and nods nervously

Ready, sound?
Liz That's fine.
Roger (*to Robbo*) Now, how old are you, son?
Robbo (*shouting loudly into the microphone*) SEVENTEEN!
Liz (*ripping the earphones from her head*) For the love of Ada . . . (*She rubs her ears*)
Producer Oh, we'll never get started at this rate. We'll have to do without the test. Is the sound coming through?
Liz (*still rubbing her ears*) Yes.
Producer Okay then, Reginald, thank you. You've been great, just great.

He shepherds Robbo back to the crowd

Robbo Will that be on the box, then?
Producer Might be, might be.
Robbo It's Robbo, not Reginald.

Producer (*turning away to face Roger*) Yes, yes, yes, thanks, Ronald. (*To Roger*) Let's find someone a bit older to start with, eh, Roger?

Roger Right, will do. (*He moves to the crowd and beckons to Mr Stewart*) Now you're a Merton United fan, aren't you?

Mr Stewart Oh, yes, have been for forty years.

Roger Right then, perhaps we can begin with you, if you'd just like to come over for the camera, we'll get started.

Producer Everybody ready, let's go for a take.

The crew prepare themselves and Christine, the clapperboard operator, comes forward and snaps it down in front of Mr Stewart and Roger

Christine Merton United, vox pop, take one.

Roger (*into the camera*) The people of Merton are finding that the day-to-day worries of an economic depression are being cast aside. For here in the town itself you'll find some of the happiest faces in Britain. No government grants have flooded in nor has there been an injection of new industry and jobs. The reason for their joy rests solely on the fact that their football team, Merton United, currently mid-table in the Second Division have fought their way through to the semi-final of the FA Cup, where they are to meet the giants from the First Division, Leeds United. It's a town where the success of the football team has had far-reaching effects. (*He turns to Mr Stewart*) Now you are a Merton United supporter, how has the Cup run affected the town?

Mr Stewart Well . . .

The crowd all jostle behind him trying to get their faces into camera range, several are grinning madly, others waving

Producer Cut, cut. Listen, people behind, could you just disperse a little, it's too crowded. Thank you.

The crowd moves away a little

And again, Roger.

Christine moves forward again

Christine Merton United, vox pop, take two.

Roger How has the Cup run affected the town?

Mr Stewart Well . . .

The crowd move in behind Mr Stewart again, grinning and waving

Producer Cut! Listen, I must insist, ladies and gentlemen—don't crowd in behind. And again, Christine.

Christine moves forward again

Christine Merton United, vox pop, take three!

Roger . . . affected the town?

Mr Stewart Well, (*he glances behind him*) it's the greatest thing to happen in this town for many a year.

As he speaks the crowd moves in behind him again, still grinning and waving but more subdued

The success of United has rubbed off on everyone.

Roger How has it affected you and your workmates?

Mr Stewart It was stated in the *Echo* the other night that production in industry has gone up because everybody's happier.

Roger And how do you see United progressing? To the final?

Mr Stewart To the final and winning it.

The crowd cheer

Roger Thanks, awfully. (*Turning to Mick*) What about you? How do the young people of the town feel about the club?

Mick Well, it's great, isn't it? Fantastic. We can't wait for the semi.

Mrs Carter (*shouting from in the crowd*) We can't wait for the end of the season.

There is muttering as the crowd parts and Mrs Carter comes to the front

Do you want to know what the women feel about it? We're sick and tired of it all—football, Merton United, the lot.

Kath (*joining in*) Yes, we've had it up to here. (*She points to her forehead*) And we're not standing for it any longer.

The crowd begins to shout in agreement and disagreement

Roger This is amazing. Do you mean to say the town is divided in opinion with the women against the men?

Gossip That's right. We're being treated as second-class citizens, taken for granted, if you ask me.

Jane ⎫
Kath ⎭ (*together*) She's right. We're not standing for it any longer.

Roger So am I to understand that the women and girls in this town are rebelling because the men have gone football daft?

Kath That's right. We're on strike.

Jane and the other women look at her, then voice their agreement

Mrs Williams Yes, on strike, that's it.

Mrs Stewart No more dinners, no more washing, we're not even going to empty the bin.

Mrs Carter Yes, and we're sending the men to Coventry if they so much as mention football from now on. We're on strike!

Producer Great, great, it's a scoop—keep it going, we'll edit it later.

The noise of arguments from the crowd continues while Roger is interviewing. Mrs Carter is confronted by a Newspaper Reporter

Reporter Chris Stewart, *Merton Echo*, can you give a quick interview for us on the strike?

The Reporter and Mrs Carter move to one side

Roger Now, girls, why do you feel so strongly about this?

Kath Well, they talk about nothing else but football, morning, noon and night. We're getting left out all the time.

Jane Yes, it's not fair. Why should we be taken for granted?

Mrs Williams Merton United may have two good strikers but they're nothing compared to us.

Mrs Stewart We've got our rights.

The shouting and arguing continues, as do the interviews as Kath and Jane walk to the front of the stage. Gradually the noise and the Lights fade, leaving them in a single Spot in silence

Kath And so it began. We girls went on strike and for the next few weeks Merton was a changed place.

Jane Our mothers refused to do all the jobs the menfolk expected them to do. As for us girls, we too played our part.

Kath The lads just had to sit and twiddle their thumbs. The whole town was in chaos.

Jane and Kath sing. The Company in the background can freeze as Jane and Kath sing the first verse and then they can come to life for the second verse to give more weight to the end of Act I

Music 6. Down Our Way

Jane ⎫ **Kath** ⎬	High rise flats, Highways too, Down our way. Nothing like Coronation Street Down our way.

The area's changed,
Not what it was before,
You must always lock your door,
Down our way,
Down our way.

Something stirs community
Down our way.
Sense of continuity
Down our way.

Down our way.
Down our way.
Down our way.

Change today.
Hear us say
Down our way.

Ooooooh, ooooooh,
Ooooooh, ooooooh, down our way.
Ooooooh, ooooooh,
Ooooooh, ooooooh, down our way.

Got no Len,
Or Hilda too,
Down our way.
No Bet Lynch in
The human zoo,
Down our way.

No *Rover's Return*
Where we can meet and chat,
Piled up high,
No back-to-backs
Down our way.
Down our way.

Something stirs community
Down our way.
Brand new sense of unity
Down our way.

Down our way,
Down our way,
Down our way.

Change today
Hear us say
Down our way.

Ooooooh, ooooooh,
Oooooooh, ooooooh, down our way.
Oooooooh, ooooooh,
Oooooooh, ooooooh, down our way.

CURTAIN

ACT II

Music 7. Overture (*Reprise*)

Merton town centre

When the Curtain *rises a reprise of the Overture (or part of it) is playing. The Company are in various group freeze positions: playing cards, standing on street corners, women with shopping bags or returning home from the launderette with washing bags, groups of football supporters, children playing hopscotch etc.*

Music 8. Downbeat Mess

The Company come to life and sing

Company
Just the other day
Everything was fine.
Rock steady, ever ready,
It's all out of time.
Yes, the other day
You would never guess
Outa the clear
We would be here
Downbeat in a mess.

(*Chorus*)
Such a lonely session
In depression.
And the whole town's feeling
Rather down, down, down,
Downbeat in a mess.
We've got to
Upbeat the downbeat mess.
Upbeat the downbeat mess.
Upbeat the downbeat mess.
Upbeat the downbeat mess.

Oh, what a mess we're in.
Nothing is ever as it seems.
The only time things work out right
Is when they happen in your dreams.
We've got to
Upbeat the downbeat mess.
Upbeat the downbeat mess.

> We've got to
> Upbeat the downbeat mess.
> Upbeat the downbeat mess.

(*Repeat song*)

While the song is finishing the Company can exit leaving Mr Stewart alone on stage and the furniture for SCENE 2 *is brought on*

SCENE 2

The living-room of Mr and Mrs Stewart. Friday evening

Mr Stewart is alone C, *trying to iron a shirt. There is a look of deep concentration on his face and he is quite clearly having great difficulty. He turns the shirt over a couple of times trying to find the best way of doing it. He burns his finger on the iron and then holds up the shirt for the audience to see a large hole in the back in the shape of the iron. He mutters aggressively under his breath and throws the shirt on the settee. He turns back to the ironing board, presses the catch and it collapses suddenly on his foot. He yells in pain as the telephone starts to ring*

Mr Stewart (*answering the phone; aggressively*) Hello. . . . Oh hello, Alf. . . . yeah, things are just the same here. . . . She's out . . . at her mother's. You know her mother—had so many face lifts there's nothing left in her shoes . . . you've got her. . . . Yes, it's a funny old situation, been married eighteen years and had only one argument . . . it's lasted eighteen years. . . . Course I'm still going to Villa Park. Coach leaves at ten o'clock, doesn't it?. . . . Yeah, she's not stopping me. It's war, Alf, war. . . . What, tonight?. . . . Down the supporters' club . . . yes, I could do with a pint. I haven't had time to get out at all this week. . . . Oh, she'll not like it but so what, I've had enough. She's even taken to getting changed for bed in the dark. Only the cat knows what she looks like with no clothes on. . . .

Mick enters

Right, I'll see you in an hour or so. Just a bit of dusting to do . . . must do it tonight, the flies are starting to walk across the table on stilts. Okay, Alf, see you later on.

He puts the telephone down and turns to Mick who is holding up the shirt

Mick I bet that's the first ironing you've done since your army days.
Mr Stewart I hardly did any then, just the parts that showed. I was known as collar and chest and bugger the rest.
Mick Well, at least your back will be cool in this.
Mr Stewart That's enough of your shirty remarks.
Mick Come on, it wasn't bad for off the cuff.
Mr Stewart Just button it.
Mick Mum not in?
Mr Stewart Need you ask?
Mick I suppose I've got to suffer another of your teas, have I?

Mr Stewart You should be giving me moral support. There's nowt wrong with my cooking.

Mick Nowt wrong? Even the mice have been sucking Rennies since mother went on strike. I could have soled my shoes with that fried egg you gave me last night.

Mr Stewart Quit moaning, there's nothing we can do about it.

Mick I'm fed up with the whole thing. They've got a point you know.

Mr Stewart Who? The women? They started it, not us.

Mick I know that but it's been unbearable in this house since . . .

Mr Stewart Don't get on to me about it. Tell your mother or Mrs Carter or that girl you were supposed to be going——(*Realizing*) Ah, now we're getting to it. I see now, it's what's her name—Jane, eh?

Mick What's for tea?

Mr Stewart Oh, don't get off the subject.

Mick Well, it's so daft. Downright unnatural. I mean, we can't expect them to feel the same way as us about United. I can understand now why . . .

Mr Stewart They're getting to you, aren't they?

Mick So they're getting to me, what do you expect? The situation gets worse every day. I saw Jane outside Woolworth's this morning and she ignored me completely.

Mr Stewart You see, Jane again. You're cracking, lad, cracking. I'm going to put the kettle on. We'll have a sandwich or something.

He exits

Jane enters and the Lights dim to a follow Spot on her

Mick remains on stage as Jane sings as if in his imagination

Music 9. Downbeat Mess (Variation)

Jane   What a crazy way,
                       What a crazy time,
                       Rock steady, ever ready,
                       It's all out of line.

                       Feel it in your head,
                       See it in your smile.
                       All loyalties and friendships are
                       Really put on trial.

                       You can feel the tension,
                       The dissention,
                       And the whole town's feeling
                       Rather down, down, down,
                       Downbeat, in a mess.

                       We've got to upbeat
                       The downbeat mess,
                       Upbeat the downbeat mess.
                       We've got to upbeat
                       The downbeat mess,
                       Upbeat the downbeat mess.

Oh, what a mess we're in,
Nothing is ever as it seems.
The only time things work out right
Is when they happen
In your dreams.

Jane exits at the end of the song and the Lights return to normal

Mr Stewart enters with an uncut loaf of bread, cheese and a very hard packet of butter. He puts them on the table

Mr Stewart (*holding up the packet of butter*) There was no butter out again. I've had to get this from the fridge. (*He drops it with a loud bang on the table*)
Mick Have you made the tea?
Mr Stewart The kettle's on. We'll watch the telly while we have it.
Mick Oh yeah, there might be something on *Sportswide* about the semi-final. There usually is the night before.
Mr Stewart You're still interested in it then, are you? I thought maybe you'd be going shopping tomorrow afternoon with Jane.
Mick Oh, I'm going to make the tea.

Mick exits

Mr Stewart starts to cut the loaf. The first piece is very thick at one end and very thin at the other. All the pieces are of varying sizes but most are very thick. He starts to spread the butter but simply tears holes in the bread with it

Mr Stewart (*shouting to Mick*) Something wrong with this knife.
Mick (*off*) Is that the one with Ziggy Stardust written on it?

Mr Stewart looks, while spreading the butter

Mr Stewart Yes.
Mick (*off*) I'm not surprised, you're using the Bowie knife.

Mr Stewart carves huge chunks of cheese and tries to make sandwiches, pressing down the bread

Mick enters

(*Holding up a very holey slice of bread*) What do you call this?
Mr Stewart It's all right. I make real sandwiches, me; not those pretty, pretty, one-bite-and-they've-gone sandwiches.

Mr Stewart finishes making the sandwiches as Mick goes over to the ironing board, lying on the floor. He picks it up by the board itself but of course the legs spring up and it is left standing again. He looks perplexed, walks round it, kicks it and then, giving up, just moves it, still upright, upstage

Really, lad, still don't know how to fold an ironing board at your age.
Mick You fold it then.
Mr Stewart Er . . . it's all right there, just leave it.

They pick up their sandwiches and go to sit down on the settee. Mick turns on the TV on the way

TV Voice (*fading in*) ... at Hillsborough where Manchester United take on Arsenal. Arsenal have a good record in the FA Cup and indeed the two sides met in the nineteen seventy-nine final, when a last minute goal from Alan Sunderland saw the Cup go to Highbury. Manchester United, are unchanged for the sixth game running, whilst (*manager's name*) is hoping that (*footballer's name*) will pass a fitness test. If (*footballer's name*) is not fit, nineteen year old (*footballer's name*) stands by. Villa Park hosts a tie that has all the romanticism of the FA Cup—(*manager's name*) Leeds against Second Division Merton United. Ken McGrath, the Merton manager is confident that his side, a blend of youth and experience, can topple their first division rivals and reach Wembley for the first time since nineteen thirty-seven.

Mick A good record! We'll soon change that if we meet them in the final.

Mr Stewart Ssh, ssh. This is it! Keep quiet, Michael. You always talk when we want to listen.

Mick looks quizzically at him and then becomes engrossed in the television once more

Mrs Stewart enters quietly, looks scornfully at the men and walks towards the kitchen. On the way she stops at the ironing board, expertly dismantles it and walks off with it

Mick and Mr Stewart have not seen her at all

If you believe in omens the Merton centre forward in that 'thirty-seven side was Alf Tabbinor, whose son wears the number nine tomorrow. Earlier this week Barry Davies met up with father and son at the Merton Social Club to ask them about the semi-final and to get their views on the strike by the women of Merton.

Mr Stewart Good old Alf, best we've ever had.

Mr Stewart They're going to be on.

Mick Ssh!

The TV goes off and there is a complete black-out—Mrs Stewart has turned off the power from the kitchen

Mick What's going on?
Mr Stewart What the dickens ...

They fumble about, knocking into furniture

Mick We've had a power cut.

Mr Stewart No, it's them blasted fuses again. I've got a match somewhere.

Mick Come on, Dad, hurry up, we'll miss it.

Mr Stewart I'm being as quick as I can. The fuse box is in the kitchen.

*Mrs Stewart enters and stands by the kitchen door Mr Stewart manages to
strike a match and a strobe flickers showing Mrs Stewart by the kitchen door*

Mother! What are you doing . . . ? Wait a minute, it was you.

Music 10. Strobo Jive

*Accompanied by the piano music, he begins to chase her round the room, the
strobe flickering quickly, making it look like a scene from a silent movie. The
stages of the chase should be appropriate to the changes in mood of the music.
For example, when the music slows down Mrs Stewart can go down on one knee
to plead for mercy and Mick can hold up cards with appropriate speeches on
them*

*At the end of the chase the stage management can appear like Keystone Cops
to clear the living-room set*

CURTAIN

SCENE 3

A street corner. Later that evening

When the CURTAIN *rises it is dark*

Mick enters L *wearing a wide-brimmed hat which is pulled down and a large
raincoat with the collar pulled up high. He crosses the stage furtively,
continually glancing either side and behind him, and then exits* R

Pause

Jane and Kath are heard off, then they enter L

Kath . . . that's the thing. That's it though, Jane. I know there are women
engineers and company managers and what have you, but it's still a male-
dominated world.

Jane Oh, you're right, but then what about Mrs Thatcher?

Kath She's just one. There aren't many other women MPs.

Jane Don't you miss Eagle?

Kath (*mellowing slightly*) Well . . . I suppose I do. But they've got to learn.
I'm keeping an open mind until I see what happens at the youth club dance
tomorrow night after that semi-final. I'll give him a chance but if he
mentions football once, that's it.

Jane I saw Mick earlier and nearly went over to speak to him. I really fancy
him and it took me ages to get him to ask me out and now this strike thing
has ruined everything. I bet he thinks I don't even like him now.

Kath He'll come running and if he doesn't there's plenty more fish in the sea.

Jane Correct, but who wants to go steady with a herring?

Kath You cod be right there.

Jane Oh, don't start, I'm not in the mood. How's your dad getting on?

Kath He's been doing all his own cooking, he's nearly set fire to the house twice.

Jane You know, some of the women are really enjoying this. Mrs Parsons, next door to us, she's gone on strike and her husband's never been to a football match in his life. She says it's called solidarity.

Kath She's right. United we stand.

Jane Get away, she's just bone idle. By the way, I met Mr Foreman this morning. He says can we go down to the youth club early tomorrow night to get everything ready for the dance.

Kath No. He's a man. We mustn't lift a finger.

Jane Oh, come on, Kath, that's not fair and in any case it's our dance, not his.

Kath All right then, I was only kidding. I'd better be going. I said I wouldn't be in late tonight. See you at the youth club tomorrow.

Jane Yeah, about six o'clock.

Kath Okay, bye.

Kath exits L *and Jane exits* R

Pause, then screams and scuffling are heard off R

Jane (*off*) Help! Help!

Mick enters R *still wearing his coat and hat and carrying Jane who is struggling to get free*

(*As she enters*) Help! Help! Rape!

Mick Jane, Jane, shut up. It's me!

Jane Get off! Help! You pervert! I haven't got a handbag.

Mick Jane, it's me, Mick, for heaven's sake, Jane. Will you get a grip?

Jane Help! Pervert!

Mick Jane, ssh, listen.

He puts her down

Jane Mick! Are you out of your mind? What on earth . . .

Mick I just had to see you. There was no other way. You'd have run off if you'd seen it was me.

Jane What are you dressed like that for?

Mick (*melodramatically*) Disguise. It could cause a hassle if we're seen together, know what I mean?

Jane Don't be stupid!

Mick Well, the whole thing is stupid.

Jane You lot started it . . .

Mick I don't care who started it.

Jane Well, why do you want to see me?

Mick Because, well because——because I don't like being dictated to. I want to be with you and why shouldn't I? Unless, of course, you don't . . .

Jane You know better than that.

Mick When can I see you, then?

Jane (*folding her arms*) All right, then, tomorrow afternoon.

Mick Right, tomorrow after——no, no, I can't. I'm going to the match.

Jane See!

Mick Ah, come on! Let's have a bit of give and take.

Jane Okay, do you promise that you'll never mention football to me ever again?

Mick (*holding up his right hand*) Dib, dib, dib. Cub's honour. I do solemnly swear that I, Michael Stewart, will never mention as much as Bobby Charlton's bootlace hereinafter to the aforesaid Jane Carter. Dob, dob, dob. (*He gives the Cub's salute*)

Jane All right, Arkala, I believe you.

Mick Are we going to the youth club dance tomorrow night, then?

Jane Yeah.

They sing

Music 11. Look Before You Leap

Jane ⎫
Mick ⎭

A cause can't be as sad
As a shoe is sad,
For a shoe treads wearily
Wherever it goes.
I could be yours, who knows?

A ladder ain't as crazy
As jeans are mad,
For jeans never stand
On their own two feet.
We're not sheep, don't bleat.
A bell ain't as pretty
As a wheel when it turns,
For a bell always does
What it's tolled.

(*Chorus*)

So, look before you leap,
Look before you leap,
Look before you leap,
Look before you leap.
If your heart will flow
Like a river deep,
You'd better look before you leap.

A cause can't be as sad
As a shoe is sad,
For a shoe treads wearily
Wherever it goes.
I could be yours, who knows?

A secret ain't as lonely
As a rock feels alone,

For a rock never ever
Has a friend.
I'm your friend, don't pretend.
A mountain smiles more
Than the moon up there,
A moon has just one face to smile.

So, look before you leap,
Look before you leap,
Look before you leap,
Look before you leap.
If your heart will flow
Like a river deep,
You'd better look before you leap.
If your heart will flow
Like a river deep,
You'd better look before you leap.

CURTAIN

SCENE 4

The semi-final at Villa Park. Saturday afternoon

On one side of the stage is the Presenter of a television sports programme. On the other side are the Merton United Supporters banked in rows as if on the terraces of Villa Park, with Mick, Eagle and Robbo in the front row with perhaps Mr Foreman as well. When the Presenter is talking he is spotlighted and the Supporters are in darkness, frozen. When the Supporters are featured they are lit and the Presenter is in darkness. During the latter sequences background noises can be used to create the atmosphere of the football ground

The Lights come up on the TV Presenter

TV Presenter ... at the Athletics Meeting at the Crystal Palace Stadium this afternoon where Jim Fox ran a mile in one minute ten seconds. Asked how he was capable of running it in such a time he replied—"I know a short cut." We have just heard that the FA Vase match between Epping Town and Blue Star has been abandoned and that the game between Fulham Fairies and Nuneaton Nancies is very abandoned. Latest news from the two FA Cup semi-finals; at Hillsborough, Manchester United still lead Arsenal two–nil, a first half goal from (*player's name*) and United going further ahead through a (*player's name*) own goal after sixty minutes. Still no score between Leeds and Second Division Merton United at Villa Park and I am being told on the headphones we can go over there now for an update on that situation. (*He pauses*) Can we indeed go over? I believe we're having a little trouble but, yes, we're going to try ...

The Lights cross fade to the Supporters who sing a part of a song from a famous musical. The front row are all on one knee, behind them others have hands on hips and as they sing they bend their knees. The singing stops. The Lights cross fade to the TV Presenter

TV Presenter Ah, a little technical hitch. We seem to have picked up the afternoon movie on BBC Two . . . Yes, we can go over to Villa Park now and the semi-final between Leeds and Merton United.

The Lights cross fade to the Supporters, who appear to be watching the match. Mick, Eagle and Robbo are clearly visible in the front row

Supporters Go——ah!

Mick (*arms in the air*) How did he miss? Oh no, it could have been wrapped up. What shooting! He nearly knocked the arms off the town hall clock.

Eagle If this goes on much longer, I shall have bitten me nails off to the elbows. How long to go?

Mick About ten minutes.

Robbo What do you bet they grab one now? That'd be just our luck, a last minute goal.

Eagle Robbo, shut up, will you? They've got to watch that winger. I tell you, he's given Griffiths trouble all afternoon. Oh, look at that, he's skinned him again.

Robbo They're going to score.

Some supporters put their arms in the air, others, with hands to their faces, hardly dare to watch

Supporters (*with relief*) Oooh!

Mick Listen, Robbo, will you shut up—burying them. Leeds are getting close enough without you helping out.

Robbo Here's that winger again. Here comes a game spoiler. Look, he's through . . .

Mick Yes, what a tackle!

Eagle Hit him again, Joe, he's still wriggling.

Robbo We're never going to do it.

Mick Belt up! Look at that. That's a great ball. Tabbinor's on to it.

Eagle He's through. He's beaten him. Go on, Mark, shoot!

Supporters Penalty! (*They boo and shout*)

Mick It is a penalty.

All cheer. This scene can be one of the funniest in the show, with the Supporters being very aware of the sequence of the football match they are watching and then being able to repeat it in slow motion later

Eagle I daren't look. I'm so nervous, I've got goose pimples on my goose pimples.

Mick Mark's taking it. He never misses 'em.

Robbo There's always a first time.

Mick ⎫
Eagle ⎬ (*together*) Shut up!

The Supporters fall silent, some turn away, others put their hands to their faces and peer through their fingers. Robbo drops his programme

Eagle Robbo, you've dropped your programme.

Robbo bends down to pick it up. While he is bending the Supporters erupt, some hands aloft, some hugging each other and jumping about

Supporters Goal! It's there! *etc.*

Robbo (*emerging*) I missed it, blimey, I missed it. Bent down and . . . I missed it.

The Lights cross fade to the TV Presenter

TV Presenter Let's have a slow-motion replay of that penalty goal that could put Merton United through to the Cup final.

The Lights cross fade to the Supporters again. The repeat is carried out in slow motion with exaggerated movements and expressions. All voices are slowed down as well. The Supporters repeat the actions as before

Eagle I daren't look. I'm so nervous. I've got goose pimples on my goose pimples.

Mick Mark's taking it. He never misses 'em.

Robbo There's always a first time.

Mick }
Eagle } (*together*) Shut up!

Eagle Robbo, you've dropped your programme.

Robbo bends down

Supporters Goal! It's there! *etc.*

Robbo I missed it, blimey, I missed it. Bent down and . . . I even missed it on the action replay!

CURTAIN

SCENE 5

The youth club disco. Saturday evening

When the CURTAIN *rises there is disco music playing. The lads, including Robbo and Eagle, stand on one side of the stage with Mick nearest* C. *Throughout their conversation he is only half listening and is obviously watching Jane. On the other side of the stage stand the girls, with Kath amongst them and Jane nearest* C. *She also is only half listening and keeps glancing across at Mick. A few girls are dancing in the middle. The girls talk sotto voce during the lads' conversation. In the original production a dance competition of sorts took place. First one of the girls tried to get the boys to join in the dance, with some suggestive disco dancing. The boys, not to be outdone, threw Eagle into the middle where, in full football supporters' gear, he did his own disco spot. Then Mr Foreman surprised everyone by doing a virtuoso spot, with the boys and girls clapping in time to encourage him. This all took place before any dialogue. It is an ideal point to include any dancing talent in the school or group*

Eagle Yeah, I always knew we'd do it.

Robbo Me too.

Eagle Just hope my voucher comes up so I can get a ticket for the final. If I couldn't get to see them at Wembley, well, I'd probably end up a cement sniffer.

Robbo A glue sniffer, you mean.

Eagle No, I'd be on the hard stuff. (*He laughs*) What about you, Mick?

Mick is gazing across at Jane

Mick! Mick!

Mick (*turning to Eagle*) What?

Eagle I said what about you?

Mick I'm fine, thanks.

Eagle Heaven's above, we're talking about the final, duff head. What's the matter with you?

Mick Nothing. I was—er—I was just thinking about the final myself. Do you think your voucher'll come up?

Eagle Cor blimey! You were miles away. I reckon I know what was on your mind. You're eyeing her up again, aren't you?

Mick Well, why not?

Robbo He's softening. "Why not?" he says. After the way they've treated us these last few weeks. I wouldn't mind if I never went out with a girl again.

Eagle You've never been out with a girl, anyway. So you aren't exactly sacrificing yourself.

Robbo They aren't worth it, Mick. They aren't worth it.

Eagle You can't let the side down now, Mick. We must show solidarity. Forget what your heart tells you, mate.

Mick Phew! What do you know? You lot think a heart is a red V-shaped thing with two pounds of Milk Tray in it. Anyway, what's it got to do with you if I like Jane? Free country, isn't it?

Eagle Oh, I see. It's like that, is it?

Robbo Ah, it's like that, is it? That's the way it is, is it? (*He pauses*) Which way is it, Eagle?

Mick It doesn't make me any less of a United supporter just because I look at a girl. That's my affair, not yours.

Eagle Oh. And it's also our affair who comes with us to the final.

Robbo Yeah, who comes with us. I'll tell you something. No gosling will come!

Eagle Quisling, Robbo, Quisling.

Robbo Aye, one of them an' all.

The lads continue to talk sotto voce

Kath What did I tell you? I knew this would happen. But we can enjoy ourselves without them.

First girl Yes, they're the ones who've wasted their money coming here tonight. They could have stayed at home and talked about football.

Kath It was just the same in our house before I came out. Me dad and Uncle Bert were at it hammer and tongs, but my mother says they're having no

tea. Just look at them. And to think I used to fancy that Eagle. I must have
been mad. What a bonehead, eh, Jane? (*She pauses*) Jane? Jane?

Jane (*turning to Kath*) I'll have a Coke, if you're going.

Kath You what? What are you on about?

Jane Oh, sorry, I wasn't listening. What did you say?

Kath Never mind. What's up with you tonight anyway? I hope you're not
pining after him again. Solidarity, that's the word. Remember women are
strong.

Jane (*quietly*) Well, this one's weakening.

Kath Pardon? Why don't you just . . .

Jane Good idea, Kath, I *will* go and have a dance. (*She moves to the other
girls dancing* C)

Kath I don't know what we're going to do about her.

First girl Next thing you know she'll be going to the final.

Kath You wouldn't catch me dead at a football match.

Mick moves over to dance with Jane. There is astonishment on both sides

Robbo Where's he off?

Eagle That's it. That's the limit. We've got a traitor in our midst.

Mick (*to Jane*) Watch out! One false move and I'm yours!

Jane I don't think Kath is going to like this. She's not keen on you.

Mick I'm an acquired taste. I was fourteen before my mother would allow
me in the house.

*There follows a dance sequence. All the movements must be exaggerated and
aggressive with the piano accompaniment emphasizing this, using short chords
in time with each movement. The boys and girls click fingers in time. Eagle and
Robbo move between Mick and Jane and face Jane menacingly. Kath and the
First Girl do likewise in front of Mick. Mick and Jane freeze and remain so
during the song and dance routine. While the girls sing their verses, they dance
around the boys and the boys remain frozen. While the boys sing—vice versa*

Music 12. Better Give Over

Company

Who d'ya think ya fooling.
Who ya trying to con.
Do ya think we're stupid.
We know what's going on.
Leave it out, pack it in,
Watch your mouth,
Don't be dim.
You two better give over.

Talk about a turncoat,
Letting down the side.
Soon put a stop to that,
Go and take a ride.
Leave it out, pack it in,
Watch your mouth,
Don't be dim.
You two better give over.

A right little Romeo,
And she's a Juliet.
Soon put a stop to that
You can surely bet.
Leave it out, pack it in,
Watch your mouth,
Don't be dim.
You two better give over.

Wanna be, wanna be in America
Wanna be in America.
Wanna be, wanna be in America
Wanna be in America.

So you wanna be in America,
You'd better go, and far.
We're breaking up the party,
Tell Maria au'voir.
Leave it out, pack it in,
Watch your mouth,
Don't be dim.
You two better give over.

(*Repeat song*)

CURTAIN

SCENE 6

The office of the Merton United manager. A few days later

When the CURTAIN *rises Mr McGrath, Merton United's manager, is talking
on the telephone*

Mr McGrath Hello, Ken McGrath here. . . . Hello, Bob. . . . Yes, we
are . . . oh, things are really electric here, really electric. How are things in
Liverpool? . . . Oh, I'm sorry to hear that . . . just wait till you make the big
time like us, Bob (*he laughs*). . . . Well, it's not every day a team like
Merton make it to Wembley . . . the lads have worked hard. . . . Yes,
you've read about that, have you? I'm seeing some of the women this
morning to try and sort out that problem. . . . Oh, yes, all in a manager's
job. Okay then, Bob, nice to hear from you. . . . No, no, we're not
interested in Sammy Lee. . . . I'll be seeing you on Saturday then, bye. (*He
puts down the telephone*)

There is a knock on the door

Come in.

A Secretary enters

Secretary These ladies are here to see you, Mr McGrath.
Mr McGrath Show them in, show them in.

Mrs Carter, Mrs Stewart, Mrs Williams, Jane and Kath enter

(*Standing to welcome them*) Good-morning, ladies. Please take a seat. Nice of you to call to see me.

Mrs Carter Morning, Mr McGrath. It was nice of you to invite us to come and see you.

Mr McGrath Well, what I wanted to do was to try and sort out this little problem—well it's not so little, is it? Perhaps you'd like to tell me your side of things.

Mrs Carter Go on, Mrs Williams, you tell him.

Mrs Williams The reason for the strike you mean?

Mr McGrath Yes, fire away.

Mrs Williams It's just that the whole town, the men at least, seem to have gone football crazy. They talk about nothing else and we all felt, the girls as well—(*pointing to Kath*)—this is my daughter, by the way—we all felt we were being taken for granted.

Mrs Stewart You see, it's very difficult when you've got a husband and a son at home who're both mad on Merton United. It wasn't so bad in the past but with you doing so well this year, everything else has just gone out of the window. To be honest, it seems as if they don't even notice that we exist any more.

Mr McGrath I see. Let me say one or two things. Do you all feel the same?

Kath ⎫
Jane ⎬ (*together*) ⎱ Yes.

Mrs Carter It's not that we're against football or Merton.

Kath No. I've been to watch 'em once.

Mrs Williams Really, I suppose we feel a bit left out.

Mr McGrath Ah, well let me say first of all that I entirely agree with you.

Mrs Carter You do?

Mr McGrath Of course, and I'm not being condescending in any way when I say that. Take for example, the players here. One of my tasks is to bring out each player's individuality. Now, it seems to me that your husbands, boyfriends, whatever, without knowing it, have tried to suppress your individuality.

Mrs Williams Oh, I never thought of that.

Mr McGrath The success of the club, ladies, I want it to reflect throughout the town, not just for the men. I want you to share in it as well because Merton United is as much *your* club as it is mine, the players or your menfolk.

Mrs Carter What are you getting at, Mr McGrath?

Mr McGrath I believe that you would like to be enjoying what is happening in this town but you are not now being allowed to, and that's what's wrong. That doesn't mean that you should have to have football twenty-four hours a day. Even I like to get away from it with my family but my wife enjoys coming to the matches just as much as my two sons. So why not you as well?

Silence

Mrs Williams But that would be like giving in. You know we've been on strike, so to speak . . . what do you think, Mrs Carter?

Mrs Carter Well, I—I don't know. The men wouldn't even want us to go.

Jane Mr McGrath, I'd like to go and watch Merton United with my boyfriend but how can I now? We can't just back down.

Mr McGrath No, I'm not asking you to. You've proved your point and you don't need to go to the men on bended knees. Why not go down to the Cup final yourselves without even telling the men? That would surprise them. Hopefully it would bring a balance back to the situation.

Mrs Williams But how? How would we go to the final?

Mr McGrath (*producing an envelope*) In this envelope are a number of tickets for the game. They're like gold but I've managed to obtain them from other clubs who would only have given them to people who have no interest in Merton, or Manchester United, for that matter. (*He pauses*) Here, take them.

Jane Hey, we could book a bus, couldn't we? Just the women, without even telling the men we're going.

Kath Why not? It'd be a good day out.

Mrs Stewart I think I'd enjoy that, I've always watched it on the telly. What about it, Mrs Carter?

Mrs Carter Yes, it sounds like a good idea.

Mr McGrath Fine.

Mrs Williams I'll get a coach organized. I'll see my cousin about it, he'll keep his mouth shut.

Mr McGrath Right then, ladies. Have a good day out and enjoy the match.

Mrs Stewart Thank you very much. You've been most kind and very understanding. Come on, girls, we mustn't keep Mr McGrath any longer. He'll have his team to sort out for Saturday. Goodbye!

The women and girls begin to exit with a chorus of "goodbyes"

Mr McGrath Oh, and—Mrs Williams . . .

She turns

Haway the lads but women are strong. (*He nods and winks*)

The Lights fade quickly to Black-out

CURTAIN

SCENE 7

A street corner. The Saturday of the Cup final. Morning

The Lights come up on Mrs Carter and Mrs Williams and a few women who are talking in groups. They are about to leave for Wembley

Jane and Kath enter

Jane Do y'know, I'm really excited about all this.

Kath Yeah. Where did you get your scarf from?

Jane Oh—er—er—off that friend who's coming with us.

Kath Oh, this Doreen, you mean Mick's cousin.

Jane Yes, the shy one, doesn't talk much.

Kath Not like my mother. Just look at her over there. (*She points to a group of women*) She'll have to go into a garage next week to get her tongue retreaded.

Jane It's great, isn't it? I mean, who would have thought? Just look at us all. Two weeks ago if Merton United had been playing in the front street we would have drawn the curtains.

Kath Aye, it's a funny how do you do. I bet we've got better tickets than the men. Can you imagine their faces when we tell them we've been to Wembley as well.

Jane I thought we might see some of them there.

Kath What? There'll be a hundred thousand there. Mind you, knowing Eagle we'll probably hear his voice.

Jane Yes, and Robbo saying: "What's happened? I missed that."

Kath What do you think Mick will say when you tell him?

Jane Oh, er—not a lot . . . I don't think he'll be that surprised somehow. (*She looks at her watch*) It's nearly half-past. I wonder what can be keeping him. I mean, Doreen. She'll be late.

Kath What does she look like?

Jane Oh, she's quite tall. Funny-looking girl really. (*She smirks to herself*) A bit of a one with the boys, I hear. Perhaps you can get her to tell you a few of her stories on the way down.

Kath Yes, I wonder if I showed her my——

Jane No! She wouldn't be able to help you on that. She knows nothing about them.

The sound of a motor horn is heard off

The women, all chattering, begin to collect their bags etc. and exit

Mrs Williams and Mrs Carter move over to Kath and Jane, talking excitedly

Mrs Williams Are you ready then, Kath?

Mrs Carter Come on, girls, mustn't keep the driver waiting.

Mrs Williams and Mrs Carter start to exit with Kath. Jane hangs back, looking off the other side of the stage

Mrs Williams Come on, Jane, let's get going.

Jane Doreen hasn't come yet. Ask him to hold on for a second, will you? She'll be here soon.

Mrs Williams Okay, love, but we can't wait long.

Mrs Williams, Mrs Carter and Kath remain a little apart from Jane

Jane Oh, I think this is her now. Thank goodness for that. (*Calling off*) Come on, Doreen, pet, you nearly missed us.

Mick enters dressed as a girl. The audience should be aware that it is Mick in drag, but the effect should not be over the top, otherwise the credibility of the final scene can be spoilt. He is very reluctant and has great difficulty walking properly. He goes over to Jane

Mick (*whispering*) I can't go through with it.

Jane (*quietly*) Mick, you've got to. If the men won't take you, there's no other way. Come on.

Mrs Williams Come on Doreen, love. Mrs Stewart has kept the back seat for us. (*She approaches Doreen and Jane and takes Doreen's arm, noticing the muscles*) My word, you are a well-built girl.

They begin to exit

Mick (*in a high voice*) Oh, yes, I do judo in my spare time.

Kath That's not all you get up to in your spare time, eh?

Mick You what? I'm not following.

Kath A little birdy told me about . . . (*She whispers in his ear*)

Mick shows a shocked face to the audience

They exit

CURTAIN

SCENE 8

A motorway service area. The same morning

Mr Stewart, Eagle, Robbo and Mr Foreman enter. They are sporting Merton United scarves, etc.

Mr Foreman What a time for the car to act up! I can't believe it—and the bloke who sold me that car said it had had only one owner.

Eagle Who was that? Winston Churchill?

Mr Foreman Stuck at Newport Pagnall! Just think, if Mick had been with us he could probably have fixed it in a minute.

Robbo Shouldn't we have phoned the AA?

Mr Stewart The time they take to get out to you, we could be playing in the European Cup Winners Cup. No, our only hope of getting to the final is to find a lift from these services.

Eagle I bet Mick's there by now. The lucky devil. How's he getting down, Mr Stewart?

Mr Stewart I don't know. He was very secretive about it, but he was up and out first thing this morning.

Robbo I reckon this is our punishment for not letting him come with us.

Mr Foreman I offered but he said if you two didn't want him, that was it.

Mr Stewart Mick'll be all right. It's us we've got to worry about now.

Mr Foreman Well, there's no use standing here blowing hot air. All we've got to do is get those thumbs going, otherwise we'll end up playing eye-spy on the motorway. What a day to break down. The car'll be all right, there, won't it?

Mr Stewart Yes, we'll sort it out after we've won the Cup. Come on, we'll stand over here by the slip-road.

They stand in a line at the front of the stage. Every so often their heads follow a vehicle as it passes them

Robbo There was only one woman in that one.
Eagle She mustn't have seen your handsome face, Robbo!
Robbo Eh, this one's got Merton scarves hanging out of the window.

The car goes past

Mr Stewart No, they were full up.
Mr Foreman Blimey! Here's a Manchester United supporters coach. Turn round quick.

They turn their backs and when it has gone past all four turn back and gesticulate after it with their right hands—thumb on nose and fingers waggling

Eagle Hey up, look what's coming.
Robbo It's a Merton bus. Look at the scarves.
Eagle Maybe they'll have room.
Mr Foreman Thumb like mad and wave your scarves at them.

They wave their scarves and turn heads to the passing coach

Eagle It's stopping. They're waving at us.
Mr Foreman The Lord be praised. Wembley here we come.

They step back and peer off

Robbo Some of them are getting out. They're coming back to offer us a lift. We're in, we're in.
Eagle What the . . .
Mr Stewart It's . . .
Eagle What are they . . .?

Kath, Mrs Stewart, Mrs Carter, Mrs Williams, Jane and Mick, who hides behind the other women, enter and stop

The two groups stand facing each other in silence for a moment

Mrs Stewart Having trouble, George?
Mr Stewart Ruddy hell, Martha, what on earth are you doing here?
Mrs Stewart Got as much right to be here as you, George Stewart.
Mr Stewart I thought something was funny this past week. Just couldn't put my finger on it.
Mrs Stewart Couldn't put your finger on it? You hadn't the faintest idea.
Robbo Where are you going?
Kath Where does it look like? We're off to see Aladdin at the London Hippodrome. We're going to the final, bacon-bonce. We live in Merton as well, you know.
Eagle But how are you going to get in?

The women all wave their tickets

Kath What do you think this is for? To blow my nose on?
Mrs Carter Yes, see you, lads. Straight down here and turn right at Staples
    Corner. If you miss it, don't worry. I've heard it's on telly again tomorrow.

The women turn to exit but are halted by the men's cries

Mr Stewart ⎫   ⎧ Heh, hold on!
Mr Foreman ⎬ (*together*) ⎨ Just a minute!
Eagle   ⎪   ⎪ Can't we have a lift?
Robbo   ⎭   ⎩ Don't leave us! *etc.*

Mr Stewart runs up to Mick and takes him by the arm

Mr Stewart Please, miss, have you got room for us? Don't leave us here. I
    know this sounds silly but I think you've got pity in your face.
Mick (*in a high voice*) Can't we fit them in, girls? Mrs Stewart?
Mrs Stewart Well, I don't know, Doreen. What do you think, Jane?
Jane We can't really leave them here, can we? And after all we do have some
    spare seats.
Robbo Jane, I love you.
Mick (*in his usual deep voice*) Watch it, you!

There is general amazement but Jane steps in quickly

Jane We'd better be moving or else.
Mrs Stewart All right, you can come on condition that you never forget what
    happened this afternoon.
Mr Stewart There's no chance of that.
Mick (*to the audience, in a high voice*) You're not kidding.

The Company enter and join the group for the Finale

*By means of an overhead projector behind the Company, slides or photographs
of a team with a cup, rejoicing members of the Company, the appropriate local
football team, or whatever the Producer decides, are shown to indicate victory
for Merton United. Alternatively, a tape-recording of the winning Merton goal
can be played as the Company freeze, before going into the Finale*

                 Music 13. Finale

Company   High rise flats,
                     Highways too,
                     Down our way.
                     Nothing like Coronation Street
                     Down our way.

                     The area's changed,
                     Not what it was before,
                     You must always lock your door,
                     Down our way,
                     Down our way.

(*Whispering*)   United, united, united we stand.
                     United, united, united we stand.
                     United, united, united we stand.

(*Singing*)   United, united we stand.
                       United, united we stand.

                       When a town is divided,
                       When life gets one-sided,
                       United, united we stand!
                       When you have to take sides,
                       When there's nowhere to hide,
                       United, united we stand!

                       United, united, united we stand.
                       Don't stand by,
                       You'll get by when
                       United we stand.

                       Just the other day
                       Everything was fine.
                       Rock steady, ever ready,
                       It's all out of time.
                       Yes, the other day
                       You would never guess
                       Outa the clear
                       We would be here
                       Downbeat in a mess.

                       Such a lonely session
                       In depression.
                       And the whole town's feeling
                       Rather down, down, down,
                       Downbeat in a mess.
                       We've got to
                       Upbeat the downbeat mess.
                       Upbeat the downbeat mess.
                       We've got to (*repeat ad lib.*)

                       CURTAIN

FURNITURE AND PROPERTY LIST

ACT I

SCENE 1

On stage: Long bench

SCENE 2

Strike: Long bench
Set: Table. *On it:* transistor radio and batteries (practical)
3 chairs
Settee
TV
Table R. *On it:* telephone, book, pen. *In drawer:* pools coupon

Off stage: Tray. *Glued to it:* glass (**Jitters**)
Personal: **Mr Stewart:** pipe and tobacco, matches

SCENE 3

Strike: Settee
TV
Transistor radio

Set: On table R: telephone directory, books
5 chairs

SCENE 4

Strike: From table R: telephone and directory

Re-set: Chairs in a row facing audience

Set: Packets of washing powder
Plastic bags containing washing
Sheets (for **Mrs Carter** and **Mrs Williams**)

SCENE 5

Strike: All items

Personal: **Robbo:** comb, tie in pocket
Eagle: dark glasses

SCENE 6

Set: Clipboard with pen (for **Producer's Secretary**)
            TV camera (for **Bob**)
            Microphone (for **Roger**)
            Tape-recorder (for **Liz**)
            Clapperboard (for **Christine**)

Personal: **Liz:** earphones
            Christine: chalk
            Newspaper Reporter: notebook and pen

ACT II

SCENE 1

On stage: Nil

Personal: **Women:** shopping bags, bags of washing etc.
            Boys: packs of playing cards etc.

SCENE 2

On stage: Settee
            TV
            Table
            3 chairs
            Table R. *On it:* telephone
            Ironing board. *On it:* iron, shirt with hole in back

Off stage: Tray. *On it:* loaf of bread, cheese, packet of very hard butter, knife, plates
            (Mr Stewart)

Personal: **Mr Stewart:** matches

SCENE 3

On stage: Nil

SCENE 4

On stage: Table and chair
            Long bench

Personal: **Robbo:** programme

SCENE 5

Strike: All items

SCENE 6

Set: Table. *On it:* telephone, papers, envelope containing tickets
            6 chairs

SCENE 7

Strike: All items

Personal: **Women:** handbags etc.
             Jane: wristwatch

SCENE 8

On stage: Nil

Personal: **Women:** tickets

LIGHTING PLOT

Practical fittings required: TV, mirrorball (for disco)

Various interior and exterior settings

ACT I Scene 1

To open: Black-out

Cue 1	Music for *United We Stand* begins *Slow fade up to full general lighting*	(Page 1)
Cue 2	At end of **Music 2** *Cross fade to living-room to give interior lighting effect for* Scene 2	(Page 2)

ACT I Scene 3

To open: General interior lighting

No cues

ACT I Scene 4

To open: General interior lighting

No cues

ACT I Scene 5

To open: General morning light effect

No cues

ACT I Scene 6

To open: General morning light effect

Cue 3	**Kath** and **Jane** walk to front of stage *Fade Lights to single Spot on* **Kath** *and* **Jane**	(Page 22)
Cue 4	As **Company** join in **Music 6** *Increase lighting to normal*	(Page 22)

ACT II Scene 1

To open: General overall lighting

Cue 5	At end of **Music 8** *Cross fade to living-room to give interior lighting effect for* Scene 2	(Page 25)

United We Stand   49

Cue 6	**Jane** enters *Dim lighting to follow Spot on* **Jane**	(Page 26)
Cue 7	**Jane** exits *Lights return to normal*	(Page 27)
Cue 8	**Mick** turns on TV *TV flicker effect*	(Page 27)
Cue 9	**TV Voice:** ". . . . by the women of Merton . . ." *Black-out*	(Page 28)
Cue 10	**Mr Stewart** strikes match *Strobe flicker effect*	(Page 29)

ACT II Scene 3

To open: Exterior night effect

No cues

ACT II Scene 4

To open: Lighting on **TV Presenter**

Cue 11	**TV Presenter:** ". . . we're going to try . . ." *Cross fade to* **Supporters**	(Page 32)
Cue 12	When **Supporters** stop singing *Cross fade to* **TV Presenter**	(Page 33)
Cue 13	**TV Presenter:** ". . . between Leeds and Merton United." *Cross fade to* **Supporters**	(Page 33)
Cue 14	**Robbo:** "I missed it." *Cross fade to* **TV Presenter**	(Page 34)
Cue 15	**TV Presenter:** ". . . through to the Cup final." *Cross fade to* **Supporters**	(Page 34)

ACT II Scene 5

To open: General overall interior lighting

| Cue 16 | **Mr McGrath** nods and winks
Quickly fade to Black-out | (Page 39) |

ACT II Scene 7

To open: Bright exterior morning light

No cues

ACT II Scene 8

To open: Bright exterior morning light

| Cue 17 | The **Company** enter for Finale
Overhead projection of slides | (Page 43) |

EFFECTS PLOT

Please read the notice on page ii concerning the use of music other than that published in the vocal score of *United We Stand* and the use of commercial recordings

ACT I

Cue 1   **Mick:** "For heaven's sake . . ."   (Page 2)
Radio crackles into life. Follow with **Radio Presenter** *as in script*

Cue 2   **Mick** turns off radio   (Page 3)
Snap off radio broadcast

ACT II

Cue 3   **Mr Stewart** yells in pain   (Page 25)
Telephone rings

Cue 4   **Mick** turns on TV   (Page 27)
Fade in **TV Voice** *as in script*

Cüe 5   **TV Presenter:** ". . . between Leeds and Merton United."   (Page 33)
Football match effect

Cue 6   **Robbo:** "I missed it."   (Page 34)
Cut football match effect

Cue 7   **TV Presenter:** ". . . through to the Cup Final."   (Page 34)
Slowed down football match effect

Cue 8   **Robbo:** ". . . on the action replay!"   (Page 34)
Cut football match effect

Cue 9   To start SCENE 5   (Page 34)
Disco music

Cue 10   **Mick:** ". . . would allow me in the house."   (Page 36)
Fade disco music

Cue 11   **Mr Stewart** puts down the telephone   (Page 37)
Knock on door

Cue 12   **Jane:** "She knows nothing about them."   (Page 40)
Motor horn

Cue 13   Throughout SCENE 8   (Page 41)
Effect of passing motorway traffic

Cue 14   **Mr Foreman:** "Turn round quick."   (Page 42)
Effect of passing coach

Cue 15   **Mr Foreman:** ". . . wave your scarves at them."   (Page 42)
Effect of coach passing then stopping

Cue 16   **Company** enter for Finale   (Page 51)
Effect of winning goal at football match (optional)

MADE AND PRINTED IN GREAT BRITAIN BY
LATIMER TREND & COMPANY LTD PLYMOUTH
MADE IN ENGLAND